Unfurled

Unfurled
LOVE POEMS

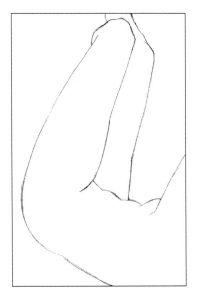

CATHERINE MARENGHI

MADDALENA
PRESS

WAREHAM, MASSACHUSETTS

Cover Illustration: A. Klein
Book and Cover Design: Mary M. Meade
Author Photo: Todd James McIntosh

ISBN 979-8-9877442-0-8—First Edition

Day by day and night by night we were together—
all else has long been forgotten by me.

—WALT WHITMAN, FROM
'ONCE I PASS'D THROUGH A POPULOUS CITY'

Contents

Unfurled

Long-Awaited Man

Long-awaited man,
you shed your clothes
like past lives,
like crumpled leaves.
Naked, you are an apple tree
in autumn, nothing left
but the strong trunk and limbs
and the single fruit,
barely attached.

Long-awaited man,
I have waited for your nakedness
as an evening waits
at the back of the day
to clothe you in her shadows,
fasten to every crag and slope
of your horizon.

Beyond this place, there is darkness.
There are cities, my love,
that loom in the night.
Columns of lonely light.

I, too, was once a city.
All my longings were roads
that scattered from me
in every direction.

But now I am the rural house,
the scrubbed wooden floor,
the tended fire.
You come to me to escape the cold.
I kiss your face and I taste
the chilled air still clinging to it.

Long-awaited man,
I am the home you will always return to.
The path you'll know, the warm
embers waiting.

The Scent of Us

I carry our mingled scent
as I leave your darkly curtained
room at first light. It wafts up
from hidden folds and blind creases
as I walk home.

It rises like a whiff of sap
from freshly cut sweetgum tree,
resin mixed with saltiness,
smoky musk or nascent mold.

I hate to wash it off. It lingers
on my fingers, in my clothes
and tousled hair.

It swirls around my hips,
a sly hula hoop of molecules
that bind to receptors in
my nostrils, then relay
whispered messages
to my still-sleepy brain.

Let it stay a little longer,
our combined scent.
Let its plumes blend
with the dark espresso smell
of my morning kitchen.

Let me breathe it in,
sip it slowly with
my coffee laced with thick
strands of white mesquite honey.
Let me lick the spoon.

Having You

AFTER A SONG BY JOHN SEBASTIAN,
'DARLING BE HOME SOON'

You show me what your camera thinks
tell me what your mind sees
from three thousand miles away.
Every image finely framed
tightly pixelated words
of the highest resolution.

I could tell you that I miss
those predawn hours, my skin
nesting into yours, feeling
that familiar nudge
my body opening its eyes
in sweet recognition.

But really, what I miss most
is your arrival at my door,
a book in hand
you picked for me,
a yard-sale find.
Or in your kitchen,
some new dish you made,
your handing me
a spoon to taste.

Would your manhood be offended
if I said I missed your artful tongue
unblinking eye
your bristling mind
more than your tumescent parts?

The phone illumines with your name.
The great relief to see it's you.
The great relief
of having you
to talk to.

Sliced Mangos

I press the peeler's carbon
steel blades
against a leathery rind,
pear-green on one side,
blushing red the other.
Peels give way
to sunset-colored flesh
slick with stickiness
that coats my hands
to the wrists.
I thin-slice what clings
recalcitrant
to fibrous flat stone within.

I resist the urge to make
a chutney or a salsa,
just a spritz of lime
on naked slices, balancing
the sweetness.

I'm thinking
you should be here, just
to taste and smell
the resinous perfume of this
luscious sloppiness.

Fruit slides between my lips,
and all I can think is this:
There is no act or chore
or ministration I can do
that does not
summon you
to be with me.

I Read Your DNA

Your DNA results omitted several things.
Without saliva swabs I know
you descended from Etruscans,
traders in bucchero urns, olive oil and pine nuts.
Your pores are seeped with mint
and sweet Lavandula from coastal France.
Your footsteps draw their rhythms from
Teutonic dance and rites of spring.
Slavic horsemen fixed the pigment in your eyes.
Warriors from Mongol tribes
conveyed your blood on arrowheads and tips
of spears. Threads from all the continents
are woven in your arteries, your lineage
pressed into papyrus mats and tooled
in clay cuneiform, your stylus just a blunt reed
or sable-hair brush. There is no water
that has not flowed in you, from Nile
to Amazon to Ganges, Danube,
Yangtze and Mekong.
All of them were spit from you
and drink you back, a nectar made
of sugar, nitrogen and phosphate:
nucleotides that I have savored
long enough to know
what others merely guess.

Banter

Words we text each other
billow unimpeded like
the gushing many-fingered hands
of mountain streams, each wet finger
overlaps and urges on the next
tumbling and repeating
pouring down the brightly lit ravine
that glows in our hands.

We try to out-do each other
and ourselves, playful turns of phrase
and double meanings
sly suggestions as
we flirt and laugh.

Why bemoan the lost art
of letter writing?
This is correspondence
of a higher art form, melding
speed and wit and love of words
leaving us breathless
using fingertips instead of tongues
saliva-slick clumps of words that bump
against each other like the frantic
rutting hips of teenage boys.

Neither of us knows
when to stop. We prod and tease
until the final text appears:
I am standing here
outside your door.

Bio for Match.Com

Nothing she writes of herself rings true:
Work she does, places she's been,
color of her hair—
all spectacular digressions from—
from what?

There are cans on the top pantry shelf
she will never open.
Woolens in her closet
she will never wear.
Too much trouble to find them.

Somewhere mice are nesting in
a mattress in her attic. Spiders
stick their cottony egg sacs
against her cellar windows,
dotting dusty rays of light that speckle
crates of old CDs and photos. Never
got around to digitizing them.

Shall we tell the boys that?
It would be more biographical than
her favorite song, favorite book,
favorite film, whether she's Catholic,
Jewish, "spiritual but not religious."
To every question, she replies
None of the above.

This is a playlist of her life:
Every morning she speeds to an office.
Every evening she speeds back.
Seventy miles per hour, and
she still never gets there—
that raw, uneven shore of herself
no checkbox could ever define.

Upon Being Kissed by a Man for the First Time in Seven Years

I want to inhale him into my mouth,
let him liquefy on my tongue
like confectioners' sugar—
    (But wait, hold back. Don't
    let him see your hunger, lest
    he think you're cheap or easy.)

Oh, but if I could just un-
fasten that top button,
reach inside a starched shirt
crisp as French pastry, feel
the arch and sinew of his shoulder.
Would it be too much to bear?

Choose instead the safe terrain
of cheek and eyelid, touch
the silver frosting of his hair—
    (How did I forget
    hair and skin
    feel this way?)

There's an old Italian saying—
Don't let the peasant know
how good pears are with cheese.

Well, now I know. Now I've broken
the skin of that ripe pear,
a thing more to sip
than eat, and now I can't go back.
I can't.
What will this man
think of me?

Beachstone123

Tall cliff of a man, weather-worn, battle-torn,
    wind-blown island of a man.
Generous as the marshy shores,
    man of hidden rivulets, life-teeming shelters,
    bright with winged life, crawling life, beauty
    as improbable as starfish.

Many-gifted cloud dweller, sooth seller, storyteller,
    if by story one includes the open book of blank
    canvas, unassembled pixels on a glass screen,
    trained hands of poet, pilot, painter, dream waker.

Will you let me tell you who I am, what I am,
    how I know you, how I see you, even now.

Salty roots of sea grasses, sand and broken shells
    beneath your feet, slender reed of a man.
Noisy face, loud face, face of crashing waves
    and booming winds, and yet
    quiet as the moon you are, and just as
    distant.

Vigilant, watchtower, keeper of the storms and high
    winds, lonely signpost, warning shot, ringed by
    greedy hunters.

How I want to tell you, how I see you, how I know you,
  from across the night waters, from beneath your steady
  flight patterns, I have seen you, charted you,
  traced your course with fingers 'cross the sky.

With an eye that will not filter, will not alter or interpret,
  I can see you, every line, every brush, every stroke,
  every paint smudge that lands upon your brow

And is there no one there to tell you? No one there
  to smooth the smudge away?
No one there to tell you
  how you are, how you are—
  spare and stark
  and perfect as a beach stone.

Fly Fisherman

You love the soft whir
of rod and reel, the icy surge of
mountain waters as you
scribble wildly with your
loops of fishing line
against the sky.

I think it makes you feel alive,
to stand firm as pulsing waters
pull and tug you like a child.

But you don't keep
the fish. You never eat them.
Something about the fine
bones that catch in your throat.

You de-barb the hooks
so spotted trout can easily slip
off and be tossed back.
It's meant to hurt them less,
but I know how they feel.

I am every strong fish
you have ever held in your hands
before you let them go.

Reception

Pulsing points that beam
across the ether,
buzzing hive of humans
passing out our twinkling calling cards
along threads of copper wire
or fiberglass. Signals race back and forth
amplified by spindly towers
wearing spiked antenna hats.

We say we have strong reception,
weak reception, no reception.
Tightrope of signals strung
between two points, oscillating waves,
ones and zeroes flung out wantonly
like unheard prayers.

We try to measure this reception,
mark it off in lines or bars
as riverboat pilots
shouted *mark twain* at two fathoms.

I would hope for four, or better, five bars
to mark how well my signal can be heard,
the one I now transmit to you, and hope
that you receive
as I am now loud and clear
receiving you.

Correspondence From a Friend

Oh Catherine.
I always say too much,
or not enough.

You bristle when I call you *friend.*
Is *love* the word you want?

What if I told you
love is only
force of habit, blind loyalty,
or maybe greed, a need
to have it all, possessiveness,
a fear of loss?

Is that what you want?

I'm not sorry, not sorry that
our minds and bodies met.
What we have is
intimacy, correspondence.
Our thoughts are in sync,
we sink into each other.

Isn't that enough?

Think about what spiders do
when spinning webs
that flash like tinsel wire
in morning sun.

Each thread is flung
in blind faith
that it will reach its mark.

For what is there for us
but trying?
The what-the-hell of *yes*
despite the certain pain of *no*?

Few eyes will see your
light-catching filaments.
I have seen you.
All the rest doesn't matter.

Forgiveness

This will be a kindness shown
to me, and not to you.
I unwrap this tightness that
had bound me to you.

The gauze falls away, stained
with rank secretion of
ancestral need.
I wanted something prettier

which only one of us could give.
I unwind myself from you,
the wound still raw and needing
light and air.

My flesh can breathe now.
New skin begins to form.
The wound's edges
pull inward, while

the mark you left
gets smaller.
Scar forms and flesh
becomes stronger.

Night at the Bar

Tonight
I am smoothed and zipped into
a fabric. I've become
a synthetic fabric, all
cinched waist and
net stocking.

I had lost acquaintance
with this dress. It feels
promiscuous to wear
what I bought to please
another man.
It tarts me up
like a dash of bitters,
garnishes me like a cocktail.

Tonight I am attracted to all
the worst types—these men
as loose as coins in a pocket,
as unnecessary as cigarettes—
I want *them*
to look at *me*.

Osiris

When I birthed you,
little did I know
I had spat out a love poem,
like the sky goddess Nūt
who swallowed whole
the burning sun each night
and pushed its jagged rays from
her womb each morning.

Always silent,
keeping all your poems
tucked between your
lungs and your heart.
Breath and beat
hummed inside
thoracic cradle,
till the day you
unthreaded raw sutures.
Viscera spilled
from laparoscopic slits
carved upon your chest,
felt as rumbles, rumbles
in your mother's
long-deserted womb.

Through your words you claim
both life and afterlife.
What others try
to dismember,
you will fuse with scars
and then adorn
with tattooed wings of birds.

Four Pandemic Haikus

1.

The more confined, the
more we see: Crown of thorns
petals form groups of eight.

2.

Hummingbirds still feed
their fully grown young: Reaching
into tender throats.

3.

Millions dead. Too much
grief to grasp. Here's what hits hard:
One whose name we know.

4.

Will we ever kiss
again? Danger lurks in each
caress. Yet—we love.

The Anjou Pear Tree

Every spring, the white blossoms
pressed against her window like a late
winter flurry.

And summertime—a green wind
in a green shade. Fruits round and heavy
spilled from flowered apron
always more than she could carry.

Even in the winter, all their creamy
sweetness stayed with her, sealed
in rows of Mason jars, orbs
suspended in embossed glass.

Every year, something she could count on.

This year, though, the white flurries
turned to green months ago.
She never noticed.

Now the pears thump to the ground
and spoil. Jays and yellow jackets
peck at ripe fruit. She knows,
she turns away, she feels nothing.

This year, a hunger she cannot explain
for black zapote, prickly pear, sapodilla,
jackfruit, bitter pomegranates.

Certainty

Sometimes there is music, but
the notes strain.
Dinner conversation is
polite, the wine good enough
to not send back, but not
enough to warm a chaste kiss
on a cool cheek at the end of the night.
And you drive home with the certainty
of nothing.

But then you meet a man
and now a shared cup of coffee
steams like a tango on a Mexican dance floor.
One look from him is enough
to clamp you like strong thighs.
And words and tears flow equally,
without fear or shame.

Then you meet a man, and now
every moment away from him
is only an intermission, a pause
to catch your breath
before the next elongated embrace
that runs from noon till noon again.

And you know you'd pack your bags
in a heartbeat, meet him at an airport

or a secret beach at night,
knowing he'll be waiting.

Sometimes, every once in a while,
comes the certainty
of a chance.

Obit for an Affair

It was born in another country, parents
unknown. A gifted student, having mastered
curricula of ecstasy and depletion,
having amassed a body of knowledge wholly
unmarketable, it launched itself into
years of steady unemployment.

It went on to kickstart an enterprise,
intended for those uniquely skilled
at working alone. It sold itself to the lowest
bidder, convinced it deserved no more.
It left no estate, no children, nothing to mark
where heat and light had flared.

In lieu of flowers, the survivors request
that offerings be made, penance given,
incense burned, and cups of forgetfulness
be raised.

Lay coins on the unflinching eyelids.
Say not a word more.

Full Moon

That first time,
the bourbon still hot on my throat
and drunk from the newness of
your touch
under a tall-windowed night
I thought I saw not one
but dozens of full moons,
effervescing from bed linens,
bursting on the tines
of stars—and you
smooth and silver-skinned
in that alcoholic light.

How many full moons ago it was
I couldn't say—
but I know you are still
full of a quality like
the full moon,
whether the thin white wafers
threaded like seed pearls
in winter skies, or swollen gold
apples bobbing in harvest nights,
each one a sight that stirs,
beauty that always startles
as if beheld
for the first time.

Somerville Night

July has the hot breath
of a panting lion.

I lie in darkness
thinking of you,
the thought of you a sweet
relief, a light cooling sweat
on the brow.

My body lies just where I left it
heaped onto the bed
like damp laundry, for
there is no grace to a body
sweating in solitude.
No feverishness
to this bloodless heat.

The night leans oppressively
like the body of
an indifferent lover.

Sunday Morning Bells

Today I drop pesos
into every beggar woman's cup
as I climb the slanted streets
to the Parroquia of San Miguel.
Thrumming Sunday morning bells
hoist me skyward to the painful
spires. They snag the sky
with cactus spines,
bell clappers slam inside
the swinging bronze.

I give my alms as penance—
para mi alma.
Metallic thuds pound me from
within, my rib cage hollow as
a beggar's empty cup.

Today I flutter from those spires,
a startled dove.
Useless wings fail me
as I fall to the wounded earth.
My eyes round and vacant as
the pesos scattered in my wake.

Today I told a man
who doesn't love me
I will fly away.

Put your ear to my chest
and you will hear
nothing
not a living sound.

Piano Recital for Vincent

1.

He almost married her, the girl he met at Harvard
fifty years ago. Vera was a portrait artist, her face
sketched in charcoal by her own hand, an image

smudged from too much handling in his memory.
The dark brows so like the young Liz Taylor
in *National Velvet*. Once again his thoughts gallop

back to her. She taught him to love Gentileschi.
He taught her to love Schubert's song cycles.
He fingers the piano keys, a piece he has played

on gilded stage and ivory halls. It was her favorite:
Schubert's Opus 89, *Winterreise*. Vocals left unsung,
breathless notes riding bareback on his deft fingers.

2.

She loved him for his tender soul. He was
not like other men. But when at last she understood,
she broke it off, returned the ring. For years he

feasted on her absence, ladled out as tepid broth
on bone china, blinding glint of silver set for one.
To speak of it would cost him everything:

his tenured podium, concert stage, circling crowds.
But when at last the laws bent and broke,
he met a man, a gifted painter. The two men

exchanged vows in open air, graying Adirondack slopes as
witnesses, stand-ins for their parents long deceased, beneath
an all-approving sky.

3.
The year the letter came: Vera, his dark-haired girl,
had found him. She wrote of how she came to be
a family disgrace. The diagnosis: "gender dysphoria."

A man corralled inside her all those years. And when she
shed her female skin, changed her name to
Vincent—her parents disinherited their unwanted

son, would not forgive, although they lived to be 100.
Vincent buried them, and disinterred old loves. His concert
pianist. His letter tore the years to shreds. Old

dead lies sprouted green truths once they could be spoken.
Calls and letters surged, then an invitation. The pianist sent
a ticket for a Schubert recital,

his farewell concert to his students dedicated to his first love.
But Vincent never said that he was very ill, would never
come. The empty front-row seat, silently

attentive to the final verse of *Winterreise*:
I came here as a stranger.
As a stranger I depart.

Almost Love

Had you not met another first
our lovemaking might have been
a tree, and all the earth below
to urge it on, to dig its roots deeper,
thicker, seeking sweet groundwater.

Had you not met another first
our lovemaking might have been
an Olympic event. I'm thinking
ribbon twirling: you the handle,
slick bamboo, and I the swirling silk.
Compulsory elements:
flicks, circles, snakes, spirals, throws.

Had you not met another first
our lovemaking might have sparked
wildfires. Grasslands and old forests
charred, homes in ruin, bed posts
blackened, fine Egyptian cotton sheets
reduced to ashes.

Instead I fill your glass with wine
in this convivial gathering,
imagining I pour myself instead.
I'm a good pour, filling out
your crystal bowl,
first to run my finger 'round the rim
until it sings

slip my toes down till I feel
the goblet's stem. Now you swirl me,
breathe me in, detecting undertones
of melon, pear and honey.
Your lips touch the rim
as I tip myself
to kiss them.

Will you sip, assess the grape
and guess my vintage?
You, my nearly love,
my nearly never-to-be love?

I Promised Not to Tell Anyone

Bowls of your famous
mystery-vegetable soup
took the edge off
late November's chill,
warmed and filled our bellies.
Flames smacked their chapped lips
from blackened hearth, while
late afternoon sun
grew soft and limp.
Single-malt scotch burned
upon our lips.

So much heat, so much soup
and scotch and fire.
Your radiant body stretched
the full length of the sofa
next to me
leading irresistibly to
the flinging off of boots, then socks
belts unbuckling, sofa cushions shifting
soft tectonic plates beneath us.

As I coiled my bare legs
around yours,
all your fullness lodged within me,
I began to drift into a fantasy
of opium dens and velvet cushions
smoke rising from shisha pipes

Then fantasy gave way
to very real smoke and sparks—
a burning pillow, flung
in our careless lust
too close to fire, filled the room
with acrid smoke.

You leapt to your feet and ran
with burning pillow to the bath.
I found a boot to stamp out
melted flaming bits of foam
flaring on the tile floor.

When you returned,
burnt cushion in your hands,
we faced each other, half naked,
sheepish but unscathed.
What could we do but laugh
at such a rude awakening.

You made me promise, *Never
ever tell a soul.*
And I promised you—
I won't.

I Give You Colors

Because I am a writer
you give me antique fountain pens,
carved mother of pearl,
Victorian filigree and gold nib.

Because you are a painter
I give you colors.

I offer you
the gesso white of my belly,
stretched canvas readied for you
spread with gypsum and chalk.

You dip into the striated pink
of places furrowed, fluted and unfurled,
apply the shade with halting brushstrokes,
glacial movement, geologic slippage
on a fault plane.

You take the faint reddish tint
of my garden-chapped fingers,
deepen it with violet
and smear it on my lips.

Appointment With the Periodontist

It's a lot like love, isn't it?
You drift on a bed of Novocain,
eyes half shut, conscious
of Ivory soap smell on soft hands
that touch your mouth,
his warm breath
impossibly close.

Your head fills with his
piped-in music,
not the kind you like
and yet you listen,
willing to give up
everything, submit
to his every directive:
Turn your head this way,
lean toward me.

Yes, you're eager to please,
you acquiesce to it all,
heedless of
impending pronged
instruments,
the unseen violence
done to you inside.

In Dreams

Dreams are never real, except
the ones where brittle things
shatter:

iPhone screens
crackle at the lightest touch.
Mirror shards tumble
from their gilded frames.

I have had days like that
when everything I touch
is ruined. Teacup goes
haywire, saucer flies as if
a discus hurled.

Wine bottles launch
themselves from lattice
racks, explode at my feet.
Red zinfandel seeps
into sisal mats,
stains the grout beneath.

Days and dreams get muddled.
It's not clear
if waking up will be the cure.

Always on the edge of the irreparable
I hold you oh so carefully, this life
this love, this everything that still
sparkles in the fractured light.

The Other Woman's Prayer

Grant that I may learn pleasure
without wanting. The sweet
aroma and taste of his touch
without appetite.
Longing without expectation.

Grant that I may make
an island of myself
from hard stone
girded round and round
by his excuses to his wife.
Let me grind his excuses
like broken glass
into fine sand.

Let me bask in the violet rays
of his excuses, while
the rest of the world
drifts away to be shipwrecked.

The Affair

When my Boston house
saw me packing my bags for Mexico
she began to suspect, but then
she is old and very wise.
How many times has she
counted my lovers' footsteps
on her creaking pumpkin-pine stairs?
She misses nothing.

I felt her disapproving eyes
from afar as I stood
on a San Miguel street
admiring the fine bones
of a much younger house.

Its lithe arched iron windows
cast mosaics of curved light
on polished canterra floors.
Lemon-tree bouquets
wooed me. Clinging bougainvillea
kissed me hard with pink
lipstick blossoms.

When I returned to my Boston house,
she could sense my treachery.

> *You've allowed strange men to come,*
> she said. *They box my bangles*

and trinkets
strip me bare
from attic to cellar.
You want one in every port!
she accused.

But no, I confessed,
I want only one:
the house in San Miguel.

At this she felt such rage
she began to will herself
to rot at her sills,
clench her roof shingles
till they swallowed the rain
and stained her plaster ceilings.

You will pay for this, she said.
No one will want me now.

The Only Question

You ask me if I love you. First
I have to tell you something
that my little brother taught me.
I am not digressing.

> He used to climb out of bed on clear
> winter nights, put coat on
> over pajamas, and go outside
> to look at the stars.

> Shivering after him, I'd stammer,
> *Stephen, why tonight? It's cold*
> *and the stars will be there*
> *at least until next summer!*

> But no, he had to see them *now.*
> Eight years old, and he
> pointed out constellations
> I'd never heard of.

> He seemed to know
> how little time there was.
> His ninth birthday, already
> choked with pneumonia, he was
> swallowing his own death.
> His agony knew there would be
> no resurrection.

I'm telling you this, because
it's not exactly love
that draws me to you.

Consider this death
that crowds us into a moment.

Consider this death
that sharpens the hands of the clock
like scissors,
snipping our time into
stingy portions, and know
it is not so strange that I
hold fast to you, as if
for dear life.

Cinco Labios

AFTER THE PAINTING 'CINCO LABIOS'
BY LUIS SAN CARLOS

Before she lived,
no one owned the color blue.

After her, all claims and suitors
dropped away like lily petals
and she waved them all goodbye.

After her, *azul anil* was hers alone.
She wrapped her broken body in it
framed her high-cheekboned face
and surly brows that challenged
everything that came before.

She alone flung her useless womb
outside her body, multiplied her organs
on her canvases, as if to say

One of me is not enough.
I will multiply myself
until you see me.

Am I too much for you?
Too much chocolate for your table?
Too much kissing, too much bleeding?

I will leave my lipstick tracks
across your face, wear my own lips
as earrings.

Do not dare frame me
in the shadow of a hulking man,
my fire dismissed as mere hobby.

Watch me climb the ladder in my long skirt
and withered leg, paint the tall murals knowing
lesser men will claim them as their own.

The color blue ran to her,
lunged face-first into her ample skirts
and then the other colors followed:
bougainvillea red, saffron yellow
edamame green, white of starched
lace, rebozo stripe,
mixing paint and milk and blood.
The square huipil, *enagua* pleats,
heavy threads and beads of her
Tehuantepec *madre*
cinched in Guatemalan sash.

All the colors ran to her.
They alone were faithful to her.

After her, the colors all lost their names
like scattered orphans. All were wordless
in her presence, lips and hearts and wombs

arranged themselves
like tissue-paper flowers
on her long-remembered canvases.

Her face and life gargantuan
impossible to fathom
and her lips, enduring, tender
and yet murderous
like five prolonged kisses.

You Come Running

I stopped at the house in Maine
where we used to stay
on Bauneg Beg Hill.
Remember that sugar maple?
You called it the Sun Tree,
incandescent yellow.
How it lit up the valley.

Inside, rooms like attics,
stuffed and upholstered with
mementos, cluttered
with your absence.

And through the back window
I could see the mouth
of the mountain path,
and you, as you once were,
bursting from those woods
with the muscled limbs of a young
wolf, and the same hunger,
galloping over stubbled ground
to me.

It was only once that I left you,
but how many times have you
come running,
running back to me?

Jealous of Time

I am jealous of the years
not the women
but the years.

Years that had their way with you.
Years that made me wait for you.

And now
as one arriving at a rummage sale
too late, picking over what remains
what you're willing to impart
of your life, of your art
of the children that you sired
when I was young enough
to forge them from my own
blood and bone.
But other women did.
And now they loom
in photographs of photographs
twice removed from me.

I'd like to think I'm more
than the places you explore
with your touch
in the dark
or the maps your fingers draw
of the unforgiving landscape
that is me.

You made my long-defended
borders shift
split me in a seismic rift.

Otherwise I never
might have known—
what it is
to be overthrown
by a force I could not
brace myself for,
could not foresee.

But now I know.

And so
I am jealous of the years.
I accuse them of conspiring
for the pains they took
to distance you from me.
To reserve you for another.
Years that branded me
the other than
the later than.

Years that alienated
your affection
and detoured your direction
time and time again
until by chance
by mere persistent chance
you drifted from your orbit

and you crossed
your final
wayward wintry path
with me.

Maiden Name

The bride tosses off her name
as if
flinging a bouquet.

Why do we even call it
maiden name?
Maidenhood is no topic
for polite conversation.
A man's name gives not a hint
of his body's intactness.

And if the bride's fecundity
is the thing,
why slather her in white?
Let her strut down the aisle
in fertile crimson
bearing sheaves of wheat
wild oats twisted in her hair.

I once walked that same aisle.
Every syllable of my name
escorted me both to and from.

Do not call me maid or mistress.
Call me by my birth name
my given name, my warrior name
my *nom de plume*

or just
my name.

Let me wear it always
as a string of thick baroque pearls,
each bead the forgotten last name
of wife or mother
mothers of mothers.

I will never unclasp this name.
It fits me, feels
warm on my neck
moves in sync
with my every living breath.

In What Remains of the Light

Our bodies whisper tales about us.
I trace the deep center line
of your chest, the slight dip
in the sternum—an old surgery perhaps?

Despite the work of years
on our faces, still
our bodies hold
our former innocence.
Protected from the sun,
our chests are pale and soft
like those of children.
Our skin shrivels lightly
at the creases, as if gifts
wrapped in crepe paper.

Blue veins and capillaries show
through thinning skin.
We are translucent, ghost-like.

But one can still detect the strong
thigh muscle, lean legs
that benefit from daily walks.

Gravity is kind to us. As we lie back
it smooths the lines in our faces
showing us as we once were,

skin clinging to the bone
eager eyes of youth
beaming under hooded eyelids.

If I were forty years younger
my head would be abuzz:
Is this man the one? Will he call again?
Will we have a life together? Marriage?

But at this late hour,
such questions fade to shadow.
I have a home, a grown child, a calling.
No need for any man
to complete
a life so utterly intact.

In this late-afternoon surprise
our lovemaking can be free
no longer weighted down
by the false hopes of youth.
It can simply *be*.

Tomorrows are a gift,
not a non-negotiable demand.
Need is replaced by pleasure.
Bloated expectations give way
to gratitude
for what remains of the light.

Sky Burial

I would row to your island
and burn the boat behind me.
Prostrate myself upon a craggy slope
flay my skin with sharp stone
flaunt myself to carrion bird
and flesh-hungry night stalker
give myself as alms
invite the sun and wind and earth
to join the feast
to eat this, my flesh,
and drink this, my blood.

And you, my ravenous bird,
while you peck and crack my bones,
your beak and claws slick
with my body's greasy tallow,
I will plant a seed in you
for you to swallow unawares.

A strange flower will take root
inside your gut.
Glossy black petals will cascade
from your startled mouth
and in that moment you will know
how much you loved me.

Acknowledgments

The author wishes to acknowledge the invaluable advice, insightful comments and meticulous edits from friend and poet Kathryn Jordan, who reviewed this manuscript in its raw form and made it better. I am deeply grateful.

I also thank the men who inspired these poems, written over a span of twenty years. As a woman in my late sixties as of this writing, I have been pleasantly surprised to discover that our capacity for love—including physical, erotic love—does not diminish with age. And for whatever pain or heartache men may have handed to me, at least I can say they gave me these poems.

"Long-Awaited Man" was selected by poet Richard Blanco as first-place winner of the *Crossroads Magazine* poetry competition in 2018 and was published in the *Crossroads* 2018 annual edition.

"The Affair" received first prize in poetry at the Marblehead Festival of the Arts, Marblehead, MA, 2018.

"Cinco Labios" was published in the December 15, 2020, issue of *Ekphrastic Review.*

About the Poet

An award-winning poet, Catherine Marenghi is the author of *Breaking Bread: Poems* (2020), the historical novel *Our Good Name* (2022), and *Glad Farm: A Memoir* (2016). The acclaimed poets Richard Blanco and Jennifer Clement separately selected her poems as first-place winners in two poetry contests sponsored by *Crossroads Magazine*. She has been nominated for a Pushcart Prize. Her poems also twice received first-place honors from the Academy of American Poets university prize program. Her work has appeared in literary journals worldwide. She has served on the board of the San Miguel Poetry Café and also co-founded Poetry Mesa, an international poetry community. She holds an M.A., B.A. in English from Tufts University, where she studied with Denise Levertov and X.J. Kennedy. A native of Massachusetts, she currently divides her time between Mexico and Cape Cod.

Made in the USA
Middletown, DE
12 March 2023

26631107R00047